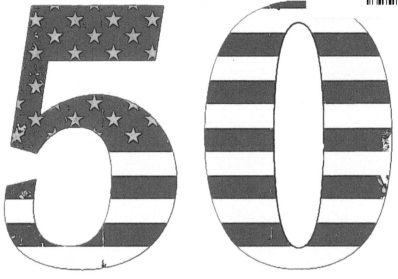

50

STATES

Travel Journal

Introduction

Do you love to travel around the fifty United States? How many states have you visited?

This fifty state travel logbook is perfect for keeping track of your memories as you tour this unique country. Traveling is not only a great way to experience new places and meet new people, but it also helps us grow as individuals and learn about ourselves. Keeping a travel journal will help you remember the wonderful things that happened, and it will help keep you stay focused on what's going on around you.

Use this guided journal log as a way to show your appreciation for each state in this amazing country.

Check off the states you have visited!

Alabama		Montana	
Alaska		Nebraska	
Arizona		Nevada	
Arkansas		New Hampshire	
California		New Jersey	
Colorado		New Mexico	
Connecticut		New York	
Delaware		North Carolina	
Florida		North Dakota	
Georgia		Ohio	
Hawaii		Oklahoma	
Idaho		Oregon	
Illinois		Pennsylvania	
Indiana		Rhode Island	
Iowa		South Carolina	
Kansas		South Dakota	
Kentucky		Tennessee	
Louisiana		Texas	
Maine		Utah	
Maryland		Vermont	
Massachusetts		Virginia	
Michigan		Washington	
Minnesota		West Virginia	
Mississippi		Wisconsin	
Missouri		Wyoming	

ALABAMA

Date of Arrival _____ Date of Departure _____

Things I was most looking forward to _____

_____

How I got there _____

People and pets that came along with _____

_____

Cities I visited _____

_____

People I visited _____

_____

What I bought there _____

_____

What surprised me the most _____

_____

Why I visited _____

_____

Where I stayed _____

_____

What I would most like to remember _____

_____

What I would most like to forget _____

_____

Highlight of my visit _____

_____

A funny thing that happened was _____

_____

One thing I learned about this state _____

_____

This was the major news headline during my visit _____

_____

Daily Happenings _____

_____

_____

_____

_____

_____

_____

_____

ALASKA

Date of Arrival _____ Date of Departure _____

Things I was most looking forward to _____

_____

How I got there _____

People and pets that came along with _____

_____

Cities I visited _____

_____

People I visited _____

_____

What I bought there _____

_____

What surprised me the most _____

_____

Why I visited _____

_____

Where I stayed _____

_____

What I would most like to remember _____

_____

What I would most like to forget _____

_____

Highlight of my visit _____

_____

A funny thing that happened was _____

_____

One thing I learned about this state _____

_____

This was the major news headline during my visit _____

_____

Daily Happenings _____

_____

_____

_____

_____

_____

_____

ARIZONA

Date of Arrival _____ Date of Departure _____

Things I was most looking forward to _____

_____

How I got there _____

People and pets that came along with _____

_____

Cities I visited _____

_____

People I visited _____

_____

What I bought there _____

_____

What surprised me the most _____

_____

Why I visited _____

_____

Where I stayed _____

_____

What I would most like to remember _____

_____

What I would most like to forget _____

_____

Highlight of my visit _____

_____

A funny thing that happened was _____

_____

One thing I learned about this state _____

_____

This was the major news headline during my visit _____

_____

Daily Happenings _____

_____

_____

_____

_____

_____

_____

ARKANSAS

Date of Arrival _____ Date of Departure _____

Things I was most looking forward to _____

_____

How I got there _____

People and pets that came along with _____

_____

Cities I visited _____

_____

People I visited _____

_____

What I bought there _____

_____

What surprised me the most _____

_____

Why I visited _____

_____

Where I stayed _____

_____

What I would most like to remember _____

_____

What I would most like to forget _____

_____

Highlight of my visit _____

_____

A funny thing that happened was _____

_____

One thing I learned about this state _____

_____

This was the major news headline during my visit _____

_____

Daily Happenings _____

_____

_____

_____

_____

_____

_____

CALIFORNIA

Date of Arrival _____ Date of Departure _____

Things I was most looking forward to _____

_____

How I got there _____

People and pets that came along with _____

_____

Cities I visited _____

_____

People I visited _____

_____

What I bought there _____

_____

What surprised me the most _____

_____

Why I visited _____

_____

Where I stayed _____

_____

What I would most like to remember _____

_____

What I would most like to forget _____

_____

Highlight of my visit _____

_____

A funny thing that happened was _____

_____

One thing I learned about this state _____

_____

This was the major news headline during my visit _____

_____

Daily Happenings _____

_____

_____

_____

_____

_____

_____

COLORADO

Date of Arrival _____ Date of Departure _____

Things I was most looking forward to _____

_____

How I got there _____

People and pets that came along with _____

_____

Cities I visited _____

_____

People I visited _____

_____

What I bought there _____

_____

What surprised me the most _____

_____

Why I visited _____

_____

Where I stayed _____

_____

What I would most like to remember _____

_____

What I would most like to forget _____

_____

Highlight of my visit _____

_____

A funny thing that happened was _____

_____

One thing I learned about this state _____

_____

This was the major news headline during my visit _____

_____

Daily Happenings _____

_____

_____

_____

_____

_____

_____

_____

CONNECTICUT

Date of Arrival _____ Date of Departure _____

Things I was most looking forward to _____

_____

How I got there _____

People and pets that came along with _____

_____

Cities I visited _____

_____

People I visited _____

_____

What I bought there _____

_____

What surprised me the most _____

_____

Why I visited _____

_____

Where I stayed _____

_____

What I would most like to remember _____

_____

What I would most like to forget _____

_____

Highlight of my visit _____

_____

A funny thing that happened was _____

_____

One thing I learned about this state _____

_____

This was the major news headline during my visit _____

_____

Daily Happenings _____

_____

_____

_____

_____

_____

_____

_____

DELAWARE

Date of Arrival _____ Date of Departure _____

Things I was most looking forward to _____

_____

How I got there _____

People and pets that came along with _____

_____

Cities I visited _____

_____

People I visited _____

_____

What I bought there _____

_____

What surprised me the most _____

_____

Why I visited _____

_____

Where I stayed _____

_____

What I would most like to remember _____

_____

What I would most like to forget _____

_____

Highlight of my visit _____

_____

A funny thing that happened was _____

_____

One thing I learned about this state _____

_____

This was the major news headline during my visit _____

_____

Daily Happenings _____

_____

_____

_____

_____

_____

_____

FLORIDA

Date of Arrival _____   Date of Departure _____

Things I was most looking forward to _____

_____

How I got there _____

People and pets that came along with _____

_____

Cities I visited _____

_____

People I visited _____

_____

What I bought there _____

_____

What surprised me the most _____

_____

Why I visited _____

_____

Where I stayed _____

_____

What I would most like to remember _____

_____

What I would most like to forget _____

_____

Highlight of my visit _____

_____

A funny thing that happened was _____

_____

One thing I learned about this state _____

_____

This was the major news headline during my visit _____

_____

Daily Happenings _____

_____

_____

_____

_____

_____

_____

GEORGIA

Date of Arrival _____ Date of Departure _____

Things I was most looking forward to _____

_____

How I got there _____

People and pets that came along with _____

_____

Cities I visited _____

_____

People I visited _____

_____

What I bought there _____

_____

What surprised me the most _____

_____

Why I visited _____

_____

Where I stayed _____

_____

What I would most like to remember _____

_____

What I would most like to forget _____

_____

Highlight of my visit _____

_____

A funny thing that happened was _____

_____

One thing I learned about this state _____

_____

This was the major news headline during my visit _____

_____

Daily Happenings _____

_____

_____

_____

_____

_____

_____

_____

HAWAII

Date of Arrival _____ Date of Departure _____

Things I was most looking forward to _____

_____

How I got there _____

People and pets that came along with _____

_____

Cities I visited _____

_____

People I visited _____

_____

What I bought there _____

_____

What surprised me the most _____

_____

Why I visited _____

_____

Where I stayed _____

_____

What I would most like to remember _____

_____

What I would most like to forget _____

_____

Highlight of my visit _____

_____

A funny thing that happened was _____

_____

One thing I learned about this state _____

_____

This was the major news headline during my visit _____

_____

Daily Happenings _____

_____

_____

_____

_____

_____

_____

IDAHO

Date of Arrival _____ Date of Departure _____

Things I was most looking forward to _____

_____

How I got there _____

People and pets that came along with _____

_____

Cities I visited _____

_____

People I visited _____

_____

What I bought there _____

_____

What surprised me the most _____

_____

Why I visited _____

_____

Where I stayed _____

_____

What I would most like to remember _____

_____

What I would most like to forget _____

_____

Highlight of my visit _____

_____

A funny thing that happened was _____

_____

One thing I learned about this state _____

_____

This was the major news headline during my visit _____

_____

Daily Happenings _____

_____

_____

_____

_____

_____

_____

ILLINOIS

Date of Arrival _____ Date of Departure _____

Things I was most looking forward to _____

_____

How I got there _____

People and pets that came along with _____

_____

Cities I visited _____

_____

People I visited _____

_____

What I bought there _____

_____

What surprised me the most _____

_____

Why I visited _____

_____

Where I stayed _____

_____

What I would most like to remember _____

_____

What I would most like to forget _____

_____

Highlight of my visit _____

_____

A funny thing that happened was _____

_____

One thing I learned about this state _____

_____

This was the major news headline during my visit _____

_____

Daily Happenings _____

_____

_____

_____

_____

_____

_____

INDIANA

Date of Arrival _____ Date of Departure _____

Things I was most looking forward to _____

_____

How I got there _____

People and pets that came along with _____

_____

Cities I visited _____

_____

People I visited _____

_____

What I bought there _____

_____

What surprised me the most _____

_____

Why I visited _____

_____

Where I stayed _____

_____

What I would most like to remember _____

_____

What I would most like to forget _____

_____

Highlight of my visit _____

_____

A funny thing that happened was _____

_____

One thing I learned about this state _____

_____

This was the major news headline during my visit _____

_____

Daily Happenings _____

_____

_____

_____

_____

_____

_____

IOWA

Date of Arrival _____ Date of Departure _____

Things I was most looking forward to _____

_____

How I got there _____

People and pets that came along with _____

_____

Cities I visited _____

_____

People I visited _____

_____

What I bought there _____

_____

What surprised me the most _____

_____

Why I visited _____

_____

Where I stayed _____

_____

What I would most like to remember _____

_____

What I would most like to forget _____

_____

Highlight of my visit _____

_____

A funny thing that happened was _____

_____

One thing I learned about this state _____

_____

This was the major news headline during my visit _____

_____

Daily Happenings _____

_____

_____

_____

_____

_____

_____

KANSAS

Date of Arrival _____ Date of Departure _____

Things I was most looking forward to _____

_____

How I got there _____

People and pets that came along with _____

_____

Cities I visited _____

_____

People I visited _____

_____

What I bought there _____

_____

What surprised me the most _____

_____

Why I visited _____

_____

Where I stayed _____

_____

What I would most like to remember _____

_____

What I would most like to forget _____

_____

Highlight of my visit _____

_____

A funny thing that happened was _____

_____

One thing I learned about this state _____

_____

This was the major news headline during my visit _____

_____

Daily Happenings _____

_____

_____

_____

_____

_____

_____

KENTUCKY

Date of Arrival _____   Date of Departure _____

Things I was most looking forward to _____

_____

How I got there _____

People and pets that came along with _____

_____

Cities I visited _____

_____

People I visited _____

_____

What I bought there _____

_____

What surprised me the most _____

_____

Why I visited _____

_____

Where I stayed _____

_____

What I would most like to remember _____

_____

What I would most like to forget _____

_____

Highlight of my visit _____

_____

A funny thing that happened was _____

_____

One thing I learned about this state _____

_____

This was the major news headline during my visit _____

_____

Daily Happenings _____

_____

_____

_____

_____

_____

_____

LOUISIANA

Date of Arrival _____ Date of Departure _____

Things I was most looking forward to _____

_____

How I got there _____

People and pets that came along with _____

_____

Cities I visited _____

_____

People I visited _____

_____

What I bought there _____

_____

What surprised me the most _____

_____

Why I visited _____

_____

Where I stayed _____

_____

What I would most like to remember _____

_____

What I would most like to forget _____

_____

Highlight of my visit _____

_____

A funny thing that happened was _____

_____

One thing I learned about this state _____

_____

This was the major news headline during my visit _____

_____

Daily Happenings _____

_____

_____

_____

_____

_____

_____

MAINE

Date of Arrival _____ Date of Departure _____

Things I was most looking forward to _____

_____

How I got there _____

People and pets that came along with _____

_____

Cities I visited _____

_____

People I visited _____

_____

What I bought there _____

_____

What surprised me the most _____

_____

Why I visited _____

_____

Where I stayed _____

_____

What I would most like to remember _____

_____

What I would most like to forget _____

_____

Highlight of my visit _____

_____

A funny thing that happened was _____

_____

One thing I learned about this state _____

_____

This was the major news headline during my visit _____

_____

Daily Happenings _____

_____

_____

_____

_____

_____

_____

MARYLAND

Date of Arrival _____ Date of Departure _____

Things I was most looking forward to _____

_____

How I got there _____

People and pets that came along with _____

_____

Cities I visited _____

_____

People I visited _____

_____

What I bought there _____

_____

What surprised me the most _____

_____

Why I visited _____

_____

Where I stayed _____

_____

What I would most like to remember _____

_____

What I would most like to forget _____

_____

Highlight of my visit _____

_____

A funny thing that happened was _____

_____

One thing I learned about this state _____

_____

This was the major news headline during my visit _____

_____

Daily Happenings _____

_____

_____

_____

_____

_____

_____

_____

MASSACHUSETTS

Date of Arrival _____ Date of Departure _____

Things I was most looking forward to _____

_____

How I got there _____

People and pets that came along with _____

_____

Cities I visited _____

_____

People I visited _____

_____

What I bought there _____

_____

What surprised me the most _____

_____

Why I visited _____

_____

Where I stayed _____

_____

What I would most like to remember _____

_____

What I would most like to forget _____

_____

Highlight of my visit _____

_____

A funny thing that happened was _____

_____

One thing I learned about this state _____

_____

This was the major news headline during my visit _____

_____

Daily Happenings _____

_____

_____

_____

_____

_____

_____

MICHIGAN

Date of Arrival _____   Date of Departure _____

Things I was most looking forward to _____

_____

How I got there _____

People and pets that came along with _____

_____

Cities I visited _____

_____

People I visited _____

_____

What I bought there _____

_____

What surprised me the most _____

_____

Why I visited _____

_____

Where I stayed _____

_____

What I would most like to remember _____

_____

What I would most like to forget _____

_____

Highlight of my visit _____

_____

A funny thing that happened was _____

_____

One thing I learned about this state _____

_____

This was the major news headline during my visit _____

_____

Daily Happenings _____

_____

_____

_____

_____

_____

_____

MINNESOTA

Date of Arrival _____ Date of Departure _____

Things I was most looking forward to _____

_____

How I got there _____

People and pets that came along with _____

_____

Cities I visited _____

_____

People I visited _____

_____

What I bought there _____

_____

What surprised me the most _____

_____

Why I visited _____

_____

Where I stayed _____

_____

What I would most like to remember _____

_____

What I would most like to forget _____

_____

Highlight of my visit _____

_____

A funny thing that happened was _____

_____

One thing I learned about this state _____

_____

This was the major news headline during my visit _____

_____

Daily Happenings _____

_____

_____

_____

_____

_____

_____

MISSISSIPPI

Date of Arrival _____ Date of Departure _____

Things I was most looking forward to _____

_____

How I got there _____

People and pets that came along with _____

_____

Cities I visited _____

_____

People I visited _____

_____

What I bought there _____

_____

What surprised me the most _____

_____

Why I visited _____

_____

Where I stayed _____

_____

What I would most like to remember _____

_____

What I would most like to forget _____

_____

Highlight of my visit _____

_____

A funny thing that happened was _____

_____

One thing I learned about this state _____

_____

This was the major news headline during my visit _____

_____

Daily Happenings _____

_____

_____

_____

_____

_____

_____

MISSOURI

Date of Arrival _____ Date of Departure _____

Things I was most looking forward to _____

_____

How I got there _____

People and pets that came along with _____

_____

Cities I visited _____

_____

People I visited _____

_____

What I bought there _____

_____

What surprised me the most _____

_____

Why I visited _____

_____

Where I stayed _____

_____

What I would most like to remember _____

_____

What I would most like to forget _____

_____

Highlight of my visit _____

_____

A funny thing that happened was _____

_____

One thing I learned about this state _____

_____

This was the major news headline during my visit _____

_____

Daily Happenings _____

_____

_____

_____

_____

_____

_____

MONTANA

Date of Arrival _____ Date of Departure _____

Things I was most looking forward to _____

_____

How I got there _____

People and pets that came along with _____

_____

Cities I visited _____

_____

People I visited _____

_____

What I bought there _____

_____

What surprised me the most _____

_____

Why I visited _____

_____

Where I stayed _____

_____

What I would most like to remember _____

_____

What I would most like to forget _____

_____

Highlight of my visit _____

_____

A funny thing that happened was _____

_____

One thing I learned about this state _____

_____

This was the major news headline during my visit _____

_____

Daily Happenings _____

_____

_____

_____

_____

_____

_____

NEBRASKA

Date of Arrival _____   Date of Departure _____

Things I was most looking forward to _____

_____

How I got there _____

People and pets that came along with _____

_____

Cities I visited _____

_____

People I visited _____

_____

What I bought there _____

_____

What surprised me the most _____

_____

Why I visited _____

_____

Where I stayed _____

_____

What I would most like to remember _____

_____

What I would most like to forget _____

_____

Highlight of my visit _____

_____

A funny thing that happened was _____

_____

One thing I learned about this state _____

_____

This was the major news headline during my visit _____

_____

Daily Happenings _____

_____

_____

_____

_____

_____

_____

NEVADA

Date of Arrival _____ Date of Departure _____

Things I was most looking forward to _____

_____

How I got there _____

People and pets that came along with _____

_____

Cities I visited _____

_____

People I visited _____

_____

What I bought there _____

_____

What surprised me the most _____

_____

Why I visited _____

_____

Where I stayed _____

_____

What I would most like to remember _____

_____

What I would most like to forget _____

_____

Highlight of my visit _____

_____

A funny thing that happened was _____

_____

One thing I learned about this state _____

_____

This was the major news headline during my visit _____

_____

Daily Happenings _____

_____

_____

_____

_____

_____

_____

NEW HAMPSHIRE

Date of Arrival _____ Date of Departure _____

Things I was most looking forward to _____

_____

How I got there _____

People and pets that came along with _____

_____

Cities I visited _____

_____

People I visited _____

_____

What I bought there _____

_____

What surprised me the most _____

_____

Why I visited _____

_____

Where I stayed _____

_____

What I would most like to remember _____

_____

What I would most like to forget _____

_____

Highlight of my visit _____

_____

A funny thing that happened was _____

_____

One thing I learned about this state _____

_____

This was the major news headline during my visit _____

_____

Daily Happenings _____

_____

_____

_____

_____

_____

_____

NEW JERSEY

Date of Arrival _____ Date of Departure _____

Things I was most looking forward to _____

_____

How I got there _____

People and pets that came along with _____

_____

Cities I visited _____

_____

People I visited _____

_____

What I bought there _____

_____

What surprised me the most _____

_____

Why I visited _____

_____

Where I stayed _____

_____

What I would most like to remember _____

_____

What I would most like to forget _____

_____

Highlight of my visit _____

_____

A funny thing that happened was _____

_____

One thing I learned about this state _____

_____

This was the major news headline during my visit _____

_____

Daily Happenings _____

_____

_____

_____

_____

_____

_____

NEW MEXICO

Date of Arrival _____   Date of Departure _____

Things I was most looking forward to _____

_____

How I got there _____

People and pets that came along with _____

_____

Cities I visited _____

_____

People I visited _____

_____

What I bought there _____

_____

What surprised me the most _____

_____

Why I visited _____

_____

Where I stayed _____

_____

What I would most like to remember _____

_____

What I would most like to forget _____

_____

Highlight of my visit _____

_____

A funny thing that happened was _____

_____

One thing I learned about this state _____

_____

This was the major news headline during my visit _____

_____

Daily Happenings _____

_____

_____

_____

_____

_____

_____

NEW YORK

Date of Arrival _____ Date of Departure _____

Things I was most looking forward to _____

_____

How I got there _____

People and pets that came along with _____

_____

Cities I visited _____

_____

People I visited _____

_____

What I bought there _____

_____

What surprised me the most _____

_____

Why I visited _____

_____

Where I stayed _____

_____

What I would most like to remember _____

_____

What I would most like to forget _____

_____

Highlight of my visit _____

_____

A funny thing that happened was _____

_____

One thing I learned about this state _____

_____

This was the major news headline during my visit _____

_____

Daily Happenings _____

_____

_____

_____

_____

_____

_____

NORTH CAROLINA

Date of Arrival _____ Date of Departure _____

Things I was most looking forward to _____

_____

How I got there _____

People and pets that came along with _____

_____

Cities I visited _____

_____

People I visited _____

_____

What I bought there _____

_____

What surprised me the most _____

_____

Why I visited _____

_____

Where I stayed _____

_____

What I would most like to remember _____

_____

What I would most like to forget _____

_____

Highlight of my visit _____

_____

A funny thing that happened was _____

_____

One thing I learned about this state _____

_____

This was the major news headline during my visit _____

_____

Daily Happenings _____

_____

_____

_____

_____

_____

_____

NORTH DAKOTA

Date of Arrival _____ Date of Departure _____

Things I was most looking forward to _____

_____

How I got there _____

People and pets that came along with _____

_____

Cities I visited _____

_____

People I visited _____

_____

What I bought there _____

_____

What surprised me the most _____

_____

Why I visited _____

_____

Where I stayed _____

_____

What I would most like to remember _____

_____

What I would most like to forget _____

_____

Highlight of my visit _____

_____

A funny thing that happened was _____

_____

One thing I learned about this state _____

_____

This was the major news headline during my visit _____

_____

Daily Happenings _____

_____

_____

_____

_____

_____

_____

OHIO

Date of Arrival _____ Date of Departure _____

Things I was most looking forward to _____

_____

How I got there _____

People and pets that came along with _____

_____

Cities I visited _____

_____

People I visited _____

_____

What I bought there _____

_____

What surprised me the most _____

_____

Why I visited _____

_____

Where I stayed _____

_____

What I would most like to remember _____

_____

What I would most like to forget _____

_____

Highlight of my visit _____

_____

A funny thing that happened was _____

_____

One thing I learned about this state _____

_____

This was the major news headline during my visit _____

_____

Daily Happenings _____

_____

_____

_____

_____

_____

_____

OKLAHOMA

Date of Arrival _____   Date of Departure _____

Things I was most looking forward to _____

_____

How I got there _____

People and pets that came along with _____

_____

Cities I visited _____

_____

People I visited _____

_____

What I bought there _____

_____

What surprised me the most _____

_____

Why I visited _____

_____

Where I stayed _____

_____

What I would most like to remember _____

_____

What I would most like to forget _____

_____

Highlight of my visit _____

_____

A funny thing that happened was _____

_____

One thing I learned about this state _____

_____

This was the major news headline during my visit _____

_____

Daily Happenings _____

_____

_____

_____

_____

_____

_____

OREGON

Date of Arrival _____ Date of Departure _____

Things I was most looking forward to _____

_____

How I got there _____

People and pets that came along with _____

_____

Cities I visited _____

_____

People I visited _____

_____

What I bought there _____

_____

What surprised me the most _____

_____

Why I visited _____

_____

Where I stayed _____

_____

What I would most like to remember _____

_____

What I would most like to forget _____

_____

Highlight of my visit _____

_____

A funny thing that happened was _____

_____

One thing I learned about this state _____

_____

This was the major news headline during my visit _____

_____

Daily Happenings _____

_____

_____

_____

_____

_____

_____

PENNSYLVANIA

Date of Arrival _____ Date of Departure _____

Things I was most looking forward to _____

_____

How I got there _____

People and pets that came along with _____

_____

Cities I visited _____

_____

People I visited _____

_____

What I bought there _____

_____

What surprised me the most _____

_____

Why I visited _____

_____

Where I stayed _____

_____

What I would most like to remember _____

_____

What I would most like to forget _____

_____

Highlight of my visit _____

_____

A funny thing that happened was _____

_____

One thing I learned about this state _____

_____

This was the major news headline during my visit _____

_____

Daily Happenings _____

_____

_____

_____

_____

_____

_____

RHODE ISLAND

Date of Arrival _____ Date of Departure _____

Things I was most looking forward to _____

_____

How I got there _____

People and pets that came along with _____

_____

Cities I visited _____

_____

People I visited _____

_____

What I bought there _____

_____

What surprised me the most _____

_____

Why I visited _____

_____

Where I stayed _____

_____

What I would most like to remember _____

_____

What I would most like to forget _____

_____

Highlight of my visit _____

_____

A funny thing that happened was _____

_____

One thing I learned about this state _____

_____

This was the major news headline during my visit _____

_____

Daily Happenings _____

_____

_____

_____

_____

_____

_____

SOUTH CAROLINA

Date of Arrival _____ Date of Departure _____

Things I was most looking forward to _____

_____

How I got there _____

People and pets that came along with _____

_____

Cities I visited _____

_____

People I visited _____

_____

What I bought there _____

_____

What surprised me the most _____

_____

Why I visited _____

_____

Where I stayed _____

_____

What I would most like to remember _____

_____

What I would most like to forget _____

_____

Highlight of my visit _____

_____

A funny thing that happened was _____

_____

One thing I learned about this state _____

_____

This was the major news headline during my visit _____

_____

Daily Happenings _____

_____

_____

_____

_____

_____

_____

SOUTH DAKOTA

Date of Arrival _____ Date of Departure _____

Things I was most looking forward to _____

_____

How I got there _____

People and pets that came along with _____

_____

Cities I visited _____

_____

People I visited _____

_____

What I bought there _____

_____

What surprised me the most _____

_____

Why I visited _____

_____

Where I stayed _____

_____

What I would most like to remember _____

_____

What I would most like to forget _____

_____

Highlight of my visit _____

_____

A funny thing that happened was _____

_____

One thing I learned about this state _____

_____

This was the major news headline during my visit _____

_____

Daily Happenings _____

_____

_____

_____

_____

_____

_____

TENNESSEE

Date of Arrival _____   Date of Departure _____

Things I was most looking forward to _____

_____

How I got there _____

People and pets that came along with _____

_____

Cities I visited _____

_____

People I visited _____

_____

What I bought there _____

_____

What surprised me the most _____

_____

Why I visited _____

_____

Where I stayed _____

_____

What I would most like to remember _____

_____

What I would most like to forget _____

_____

Highlight of my visit _____

_____

A funny thing that happened was _____

_____

One thing I learned about this state _____

_____

This was the major news headline during my visit _____

_____

Daily Happenings _____

_____

_____

_____

_____

_____

_____

TEXAS

Date of Arrival _____ Date of Departure _____

Things I was most looking forward to _____

_____

How I got there _____

People and pets that came along with _____

_____

Cities I visited _____

_____

People I visited _____

_____

What I bought there _____

_____

What surprised me the most _____

_____

Why I visited _____

_____

Where I stayed _____

_____

What I would most like to remember _____

_____

What I would most like to forget _____

_____

Highlight of my visit _____

_____

A funny thing that happened was _____

_____

One thing I learned about this state _____

_____

This was the major news headline during my visit _____

_____

Daily Happenings _____

_____

_____

_____

_____

_____

_____

_____

UTAH

Date of Arrival _____ Date of Departure _____

Things I was most looking forward to _____

_____

How I got there _____

People and pets that came along with _____

_____

Cities I visited _____

_____

People I visited _____

_____

What I bought there _____

_____

What surprised me the most _____

_____

Why I visited _____

_____

Where I stayed _____

_____

What I would most like to remember _____

_____

What I would most like to forget _____

_____

Highlight of my visit _____

_____

A funny thing that happened was _____

_____

One thing I learned about this state _____

_____

This was the major news headline during my visit _____

_____

Daily Happenings _____

_____

_____

_____

_____

_____

_____

VERMONT

Date of Arrival _____ Date of Departure _____

Things I was most looking forward to _____

_____

How I got there _____

People and pets that came along with _____

_____

Cities I visited _____

_____

People I visited _____

_____

What I bought there _____

_____

What surprised me the most _____

_____

Why I visited _____

_____

Where I stayed _____

_____

What I would most like to remember _____

_____

What I would most like to forget _____

_____

Highlight of my visit _____

_____

A funny thing that happened was _____

_____

One thing I learned about this state _____

_____

This was the major news headline during my visit _____

_____

Daily Happenings _____

_____

_____

_____

_____

_____

_____

VIRGINIA

Date of Arrival _____ Date of Departure _____

Things I was most looking forward to _____

_____

How I got there _____

People and pets that came along with _____

_____

Cities I visited _____

_____

People I visited _____

_____

What I bought there _____

_____

What surprised me the most _____

_____

Why I visited _____

_____

Where I stayed _____

_____

What I would most like to remember _____

_____

What I would most like to forget _____

_____

Highlight of my visit _____

_____

A funny thing that happened was _____

_____

One thing I learned about this state _____

_____

This was the major news headline during my visit _____

_____

Daily Happenings _____

_____

_____

_____

_____

_____

_____

WASHINGTON

Date of Arrival _____ Date of Departure _____

Things I was most looking forward to _____

_____

How I got there _____

People and pets that came along with _____

_____

Cities I visited _____

_____

People I visited _____

_____

What I bought there _____

_____

What surprised me the most _____

_____

Why I visited _____

_____

Where I stayed _____

_____

What I would most like to remember _____

_____

What I would most like to forget _____

_____

Highlight of my visit _____

_____

A funny thing that happened was _____

_____

One thing I learned about this state _____

_____

This was the major news headline during my visit _____

_____

Daily Happenings _____

_____

_____

_____

_____

_____

_____

_____

WEST VIRGINIA

Date of Arrival _____ Date of Departure _____

Things I was most looking forward to _____

_____

How I got there _____

People and pets that came along with _____

_____

Cities I visited _____

_____

People I visited _____

_____

What I bought there _____

_____

What surprised me the most _____

_____

Why I visited _____

_____

Where I stayed _____

_____

What I would most like to remember _____

_____

What I would most like to forget _____

_____

Highlight of my visit _____

_____

A funny thing that happened was _____

_____

One thing I learned about this state _____

_____

This was the major news headline during my visit _____

_____

Daily Happenings _____

_____

_____

_____

_____

_____

_____

WISCONSIN

Date of Arrival _____ Date of Departure _____

Things I was most looking forward to _____

_____

How I got there _____

People and pets that came along with _____

_____

Cities I visited _____

_____

People I visited _____

_____

What I bought there _____

_____

What surprised me the most _____

_____

Why I visited _____

_____

Where I stayed _____

_____

What I would most like to remember _____

_____

What I would most like to forget _____

_____

Highlight of my visit _____

_____

A funny thing that happened was _____

_____

One thing I learned about this state _____

_____

This was the major news headline during my visit _____

_____

Daily Happenings _____

_____

_____

_____

_____

_____

WYOMING

Date of Arrival _____ Date of Departure _____

Things I was most looking forward to _____

_____

How I got there _____

People and pets that came along with _____

_____

Cities I visited _____

_____

People I visited _____

_____

What I bought there _____

_____

What surprised me the most _____

_____

Why I visited _____

_____

Where I stayed _____

_____

What I would most like to remember _____

_____

What I would most like to forget _____

_____

Highlight of my visit _____

_____

A funny thing that happened was _____

_____

One thing I learned about this state _____

_____

This was the major news headline during my visit _____

_____

Daily Happenings _____

_____

_____

_____

_____

_____

_____

OTHER MEMORIES

_____

_____

_____

_____

_____

_____

_____

_____

_____

_____

_____

_____

_____

_____

_____

Made in the USA
Las Vegas, NV
31 August 2021